STEP-UP HISTORY

The Indus Valley Civilisation

Rhona Dick

Evans

Published by Evans Brothers Limited
2A Portman Mansions
Chiltern Street
London W1U 6NR

© Evans Brothers Limited 2006

Produced for Evans Brothers Limited by
White-Thomson Publishing Ltd,
Bridgewater Business Centre,
210 High Street,
Lewes, East Sussex BN7 2NH

Printed in Hong Kong by New Era Printing Co. Ltd.

Project manager: Ruth Nason

Designer: Helen Nelson, Jet the Dog

Consultants: Rosie Turner-Bisset, Reader in
Education and Director of Learning and
Teaching, Faculty of Education, University of
Middlesex; Ilona Aronovsky, History Education
Consultancy.

British Library Cataloguing in Publication Data

Dick, Rhona

The Indus valley civilisation - (Step-up history)
1. Indus civilization - Juvenile literature
I. Title
934

ISBN-10: 0 237 530414

13 - digit ISBN (from 1 Jan 2007)

978 0 237 53041 9

Picture acknowledgements:

Corbis Images: pages 6 (Gianni Dagli Orti), 8t
(Bojan Brecelj), 21t (Archivo Iconografico, S.A.), 21r
(Diego Lezama Orezzoli), 25t (Bettmann), 25b (Nik
Wheeler); harappa.com: cover and pages 5, 7, 8b,
9l, 9r, 10, 11t, 11b, 12l, 13t, 13b, 14t, 14b, 15l,
15r, 16, 17, 18, 19t, 19b, 21b, 22t, 22c, 22b, 23,
26l, 26r, 27l, 27r; Topfoto: page 12r.

Maps by Helen Nelson.

Contents

Where on earth is the Indus Valley?

The Indus Valley is the area of land through which the River Indus flows. The river has its source in Tibet and from there it flows through Kashmir and modern-day Pakistan to the Arabian Sea.

Find a map of the area in an atlas. You will see that several large cities are built close to the river's banks.

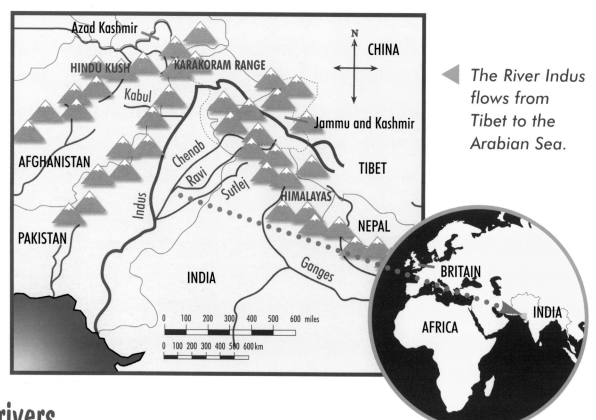

The River Indus flows from Tibet to the Arabian Sea.

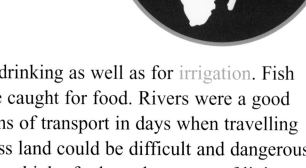

Settlements near rivers

Long, long ago people also built their settlements near rivers. The ancient Egyptian civilisation was centred on the River Nile. The people of Mesopotamia lived between the Tigris and Euphrates rivers in the country that we now call Iraq. See if you can find these places on a map.

Living close to a river had many advantages. The water could be used for cooking, washing and drinking as well as for irrigation. Fish were caught for food. Rivers were a good means of transport in days when travelling across land could be difficult and dangerous. Try to think of other advantages of living close to a river.

You have to be careful not to build your home too close to the riverbank. Why do you think that is?

Flood waters

On the map on page 4, find the Himalayas. These high mountains have lots of snow. In summer, when the snow melts, the water finds its way into the rivers and sometimes they flood. Monsoon winds also bring heavy rain and this can cause more flooding. But when the flood waters subside, they leave a layer of silt, which is very fertile and good for growing crops.

The Indus Valley civilisation

About 6,000 years ago people thought that it would be good to live close to the Indus and its tributaries. They began to build their villages, towns and cities there.

The civilisation spread over a huge area and many of the settlements were hundreds of kilometres apart. Even so, archaeologists have found similar artefacts in several of them. Long-distance trade of valuable goods was very important.

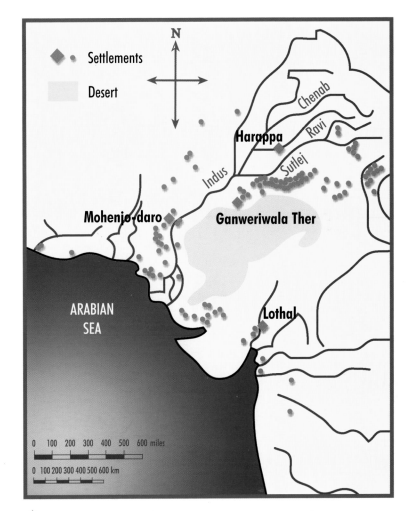

These are some of the important settlements of the Indus Valley civilisation. The civilisation covered an area of land more than four times the size of Britain.

▶ More than 2,000 seals like this have been found in the Indus Valley. Traders would have used these seals to mark their goods.

In the rest of this book you will learn more about the people who lived in the Indus Valley so long ago.

When did the civilisation flourish?

What is a civilisation?

A civilisation comes into being when people begin to live and work more closely with others for everyone's benefit. We know that four great civilisations existed at about the same time: Ancient Egypt, Mesopotamia, Ancient China and the Indus Valley.

▲ *This ancient Egyptian painting was made about 2100 or 2000 BC, the same time as the Indus Valley civilisation was reaching its height.*

When did the Indus Valley civilisation begin?

When we think of a period of history such as Tudor times, for example, we can give exact dates for the start and end of the period. The dates of the Tudor period correspond to the dates of the first and last monarchs of the House of Tudor. But we can give only approximate dates for the Indus Valley civilisation.

About 9,000 years ago people lived in the hills, west of the Indus Valley. They kept animals, but did not farm very much. Over the next 1,000 years they began to cultivate the land and grow crops.

People gradually learned that the alluvial soil on the flood plains of the Indus Valley was rich in nutrients and gave better crop yields. So, about 4000-3200 BC, the people began to farm this land. How do you think they found out about the soil?

At the time we think of as the beginning of the Indus Valley civilisation, about 2600 BC, some people were already living in villages and towns. Some of these, like Harappa, developed into cities. New cities were built too. Mohenjo-daro might have been a new city. How do you think people's lives changed when they started to build larger cities?

The civilisation grew and flourished as people developed new technology and skills to live in an urban environment. Then, after about 1900 BC, there is evidence of decline.

▲ At the Indus Valley city of Harappa archaeologists found a large public well and public bathing areas, which may also have been used for washing clothes.

▶ *There is disagreement about how the Indus Valley civilisation started. It was probably a combination of these ideas.*

I believe people with new ideas took over more lands, by force if they had to!

I believe there was no invasion. The people who lived there gradually developed their skills.

Make a timeline

Draw a timeline on a strip of paper at least one metre long. Use a scale of 2cm represents 100 years.

Find out the dates of the ancient Egyptian and the Mesopotamian civilisations. Then mark these and the Indus Valley civilisation on the timeline. Use three different colours, as they will overlap. Now mark on other historical periods you have studied.

Meet an archaeologist

We know about the Indus Valley civilisation from the work of archaeologists. For this book, an archaeologist answered some questions about her work.

What do archaeologists do?

We find out how people lived long ago by studying remains found where the people lived. We might find buildings, pottery, tools and natural materials such as bones, seeds and pollen. All these help us to learn about civilisations like the Indus Valley civilisation.

▲ An archaeologist tries to piece together some bones from an excavation.

▲ These archaeologists in the Indus Valley are carefully digging up a storage jar.

How do you know where to dig?

It's like being a detective – we look for clues. In hot, dry places houses were built of mud-brick. They needed to be rebuilt every few decades. Old houses were flattened and new ones built on top. Eventually a mound formed. So a mound is one clue.

What tools do you use?

We have to dig very carefully with small trowels. Sometimes we use brushes to clean away dirt. We use cameras and paper and pencils to record everything.

When did archaeologists begin work in the Indus Valley?

Archaeologists first excavated Harappa and Mohenjo-daro about 80 years ago. They were the two largest cities of the Indus civilisation. Sir Mortimer Wheeler excavated them at the end of the 1940s. Now Mohenjo-daro is a UNESCO heritage site, so no more digs can take place there.

What did they find?

Apart from buildings, the archaeologists found seals, jewellery, statues, tools, pottery, and also graves containing personal possessions. We can make deductions from all these artefacts. Again, it is like being a detective!

What happens when you find something?

Imagine how thrilling it is to find something that has been buried for thousands of years! The artefacts are cleaned, studied and photographed. We can often date them from their style, or how deep underground they were found. We make careful plans of the buildings and the findspots.

What happens when you have finished digging?

Important finds usually go to local museums. Pottery sherds are sometimes reburied on the site. Eventually we write a book describing our excavations.

▶ A model of a begging dog, found at Harappa. It is 7cm high.

◀ A necklace from Mohenjo-daro. Each green bead is about 2cm long.

What would you ask?

Choose one of the two artefacts above, which archaeologists found in the Indus Valley. Write down three questions you would like to ask about it.

Visiting Mohenjo-daro: the upper town

Many Indus cities had walled areas. Some of these were built much higher than the rest of the town. Archaeologists thought that these areas could be citadels, with palaces and centres of administration, but there is not much evidence to go on.

There are many large buildings on the Upper Mound, or upper town area, in Mohenjo-daro. Some must have been very important.

▲ *This is the Upper Mound at Mohenjo-daro. The site can never be fully excavated because the Buddhist temple on the top is protected. Also, the water table has risen and this prevents deep excavation.*

Check the sizes

Which of the three buildings described on page 11 would fit into your school hall? Measure out their sizes in the playground. Try to imagine how large the Upper Mound was.

Calculate how much water would fill the Great Bath. (1 cubic metre = 1000 litres.)

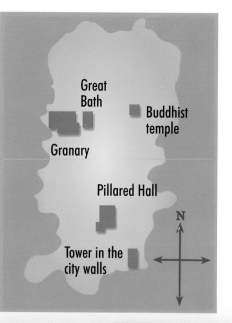

Great Bath

Buddhist temple

Granary

Pillared Hall

N

Tower in the city walls

◀ *The area of the Upper Mound is about 350 metres from north to south and 180 metres from west to east. The photograph above is taken from the east.*

The Great Bath

In the middle of one building is a large pool, about 7m wide, 12m long and 2.5m deep. It is sealed with bitumen to make it watertight and its floor slopes down to a large drainage hole in one corner. It is known as the 'Great Bath'. Some people thought that it might have been used in religious ceremonies.

Along the east side of the building are eight small rooms with drains. One room has a well and another has a staircase to an upper level. Few artefacts were found here.

▲ *At the north and south ends of the Great Bath there are wide staircases. Here you can see the staircase at the south end.*

The Granary

The building called the Granary measures 50m x 27m. Not all archaeologists believe that it was used to store grain, as no evidence of any has been found. Some people think it could have been a storeroom for valuable trade goods.

▼ *The square blocks on this mound are the Granary.*

The Pillared Hall

Another large building, called the Pillared Hall, measures 27m x 27m. Blocks of large bricks stand in rows and might have supported a wooden roof. In later years this large hall was divided by rows of walls, paving and some small rooms. Several artefacts were found here, including beads, jars and shells.

Exploring the lower town

Not far from the Upper Mound is the lower town of Mohenjo-daro. Imagine walking along its main street. It is 11m wide and runs north-south. It seems likely that the whole town was planned on a grid, with the alleys running east-west. We cannot know for sure because the whole site has not been excavated.

▼ An alley in the lower town.

What are the houses like?

The walls of the buildings are made of brick. They are very high, but the top sections have been added at a later date; they are not so well built. Were new houses built on top of old ones? There are some very big houses and some smaller ones side by side. Most of the walls along the main roads have no windows or doors.

Inside a house

Turn into an alley and enter a house. It has a courtyard with rooms leading off. There is a staircase in the corner. There is also a well, about 15m deep, lined with wedge-shaped bricks.

▼ An archaeologist investigates a well.

It's impossible to tell what most of the rooms were for, but one appears to have been a bathroom as there is a brick platform and a drain. In another room there is a brick toilet.

Back outside

What happens to the bathwater? Outside, a brick chute leads to a drain in the middle of the lane. You can follow the drain, which is covered with slabs, until it reaches the main road. Here it feeds into another drain.

There are drains on both sides of this wide road, and manholes so that the drains could be unblocked. Some houses have brick containers built on the side. Could these have been 'dustbins'?

Other buildings

Some of the smaller buildings here might have been shops or workshops. One seems to have a kiln. Nearby there is a sort of alcove with a well, which was probably for public use.

◀ Houses had a bathing area with a water-tight floor and a drain.

▼ A street drain covered with stone slabs.

Dealing with waste

Look at books about Tudor England to find out what people did with their rubbish. Draw pictures showing the differences between waste disposal in the Indus Valley, Tudor England and your home.

Everyday life in the Indus Valley

What did people eat?

Archaeologists found burnt seeds of plants including cotton, sesame, wheat and barley. These would probably have been grown on the flood plains. The last three types of plants mentioned would provide food.

There is evidence from seals, decorated pots and bones that people fished and kept animals like bulls and goats, and they hunted wild animals. They ate fruit as well; there is a picture of a fig tree on a pot, and date stones have been found. The dates might have been imported, not grown in the Indus Valley.

▼ *This archaeologist is taking away a sample of earth from a hearth. He will examine it to find evidence of the food people cooked.*

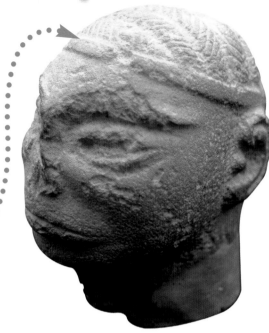

▶ *Statues are a source of information about what people wore. This man has a headband called a fillet.*

Fashion

We know that cotton was grown and sheep provided wool. Conditions in the Indus Valley meant that natural materials made from cotton and wool would not survive, so our knowledge of fashion comes from a few small statues and decorated pots.

Some statues show men with fillets around their heads. This might mean they were important. Some men had beards and longer hair was worn in a bun, perhaps to represent a warrior. Beautiful jewellery and beads made of semi-precious stones and metals have been found.

These pots were found in a grave. The tallest vase is 63cm high, and the large globe-shaped one is 44cm high.

Whistles like these are the only musical instruments that have survived. Some were bird-shaped like the one on the right.

Earning a living

From the artefacts that have been found, work out what some of the people did. For example, pots were made by potters.

In this organised society there must have been people employed for the benefit of the whole community: for example, people who maintained the drains and roads. Think of some other jobs like these.

Other people would have been farmers or fishermen. The highly developed technology suggests that there were also engineers.

Leisure time

What did people do in their spare time? We know that they had dice, board games and small polished marbles. For music they played whistles and maybe there were harps. Toys for children included clay carts, animals with moveable heads and rattles.

Sorting objects

From information in this book, make a list of artefacts that have been found. Sort them into groups in different ways: e.g. according to their use, or the materials they are made from.

Weights and measures

Why do you think that sets of weights like these were made of stone rather than clay?

When you remember that the Indus Valley civilisation flourished more than 4,000 years ago, it is sometimes hard to imagine that many of the people were highly skilled mathematicians and engineers.

Weights

Archaeologists have found identical cube-shaped weights, made of stone, in many of the cities. The smallest weight found was about 0.85g. Each subsequent weight was doubled until the stone weighed about 54g. At weights above this the pattern was not so obvious.

Two copper pans have been found, which might have been used with the weights. Each pan has three holes near the edge. The pans were probably hung from a piece of wood to make a balance, but the wood has not survived.

We know that Indus Valley people traded throughout the region and also in Mesopotamia. See if you can explain why it was important that there was a common system of weights.

Measures

In three major cities, some 'rulers' have been found:

- On rulers found in Lothal, the distance between divisions was 1.7mm.
- On the Harappan ruler the divisions were 9.3mm apart.

- On the rulers found in Mohenjo-daro the distance between divisions was 6.7mm. Every five divisions were marked with a small circle, and every ten with a larger circle.

The differences in these rulers might have something to do with their purpose. Which occupations can you think of that would need very accurate measurements?

Compare rulers

Use three strips of card about 2cm wide to make the three different rulers. For more accuracy, only mark every five divisions. For example, the Lothal ruler would have marks at 0mm, 8.5mm, 17mm, 25.5mm, etc.

Use the rulers to measure some things in the room and record the different measurements.

How skilled were the people who made the original rulers?

▶ *Archaeologists have stripped away the surrounding material to show this cylinder-shaped well.*

Bricks

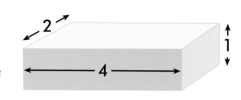

All bricks were made in the same ratio of 4:2:1, although different-sized bricks have been found. Bigger ones were used to build the city walls and smaller ones for houses. People in Mohenjo-daro and Harappa were the first to realise that fired bricks baked in a kiln were more durable than sun-dried bricks. Both kinds of brick were used in these cities.

What other skills do you think the people needed?

Playing detective

Archaeologists do not always agree about the purpose of things they have found. They try to work out what an object is from:

- its size and shape;
- what it is made of;
- where it was found.

If you look closely at some of the artefacts here and think carefully, you might put forward some different but equally possible interpretations of what they are.

Deductions

Archaeologists have experience of artefacts from other civilisations. In several houses in Mohenjo-daro they found some tiny pots, less than 4cm high, with very narrow openings. Lying nearby were some copper or bronze rods, each about 10cm long. The archaeologists thought the pots were probably for eye make-up, because they were similar to pots used in this way elsewhere.

The priest-king

When archaeologists found the statue below at Mohenjo-daro, they recognised the trefoil pattern on the cloak. In Mesopotamia and Egypt this symbol was linked to religion and astrology. So perhaps the statue might represent a god or an important person. Archaeologists called the statue the 'priest-king'.

The statue of the 'priest-king' is 17.5cm high. The priest-king is wearing a fillet with a jewel at the centre.

More examples

In many cities archaeologists found piles of clay spheres. These were solid, formed by hand and lightly baked. There were three different sizes. The smallest was about 2.5cm in diameter. The next weighed 150g and the largest 300g. In Mohenjo-daro the spheres were found near the walls of the Upper Mound. What do you think they were for? Archaeologists decided that they were probably sling-shots because of their size and the findspots.

▲ *This ring stone found at Harappa was cleaned and carried to the museum there. Archaeologists think that it may have been a base for a pillar.*

▼ *On the other side of this terracotta container there is a slot for a door. No lid was found. What could it have been used for?*

What could these be?

1. Found in drains and bathrooms, these objects are made of rough terracotta. Usually triangular, they measure about 10cm across.

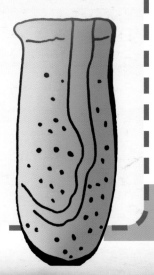

2. Found in houses, these flat-based terracotta containers, measuring between 45mm and 39cm, have holes punched all over them.

The written word

The beginning of writing

People have not always used writing. It was only when there was a need to record information, perhaps for trade, that the earliest forms of writing began. That was probably in Mesopotamia around 3000 BC.

Pictograms and ideograms

Early writing used pictograms, pictures that represent objects. Gradually, as people wanted to communicate more complicated ideas, they developed ideograms. Ideograms are combinations of pictograms, or pictograms that have been slightly altered. Later still people used rebuses. A rebus is a picture of something whose name sounds

▲ *The top left pictogram represents a hunter. Can you identify the others? The last one says when the hunter goes hunting.*

like the word you want to write: for example, a picture of a deer for 'dear'. Writers need to show whether they are using the picture for the object or for the sound. Why is it difficult to decode a rebus if you do not know what language was used?

▼ *Do you think ideograms are quicker to write than pictograms?*

Horizon

Sky

Rain

Fire

Water

Mountain

Ways of writing

(1) Draw some pictograms of familiar objects.
(2) Draw some ideograms.
(3) Write your name using pictograms, ideograms and rebuses.

When we write, we use letters which stand for sounds. By combining the 26 letters of our alphabet we can write any word in our language. That is an efficient way of communicating, even though it can be quite hard to learn.

To write using ideograms you need hundreds of symbols. A written language like that is very difficult to learn. Ancient Egyptian hieroglyphs and Chinese and Japanese scripts are examples of ideograms.

◀ Ancient Egyptian writing consisted of ideograms called hieroglyphs.

▼ This is an example of cuneiform writing from Mesopotamia.

Decoding the ancient texts

For centuries people could not read the ancient Egyptian hieroglyphs. The break-through came when the Rosetta Stone was found in 1799. The same text was written on the stone in Greek, modern Egyptian and hieroglyphs. See if you can say how this helped people to translate the hieroglyphs.

In the 1830s a large rock carving in Persia helped a British army officer, Sir Henry Rawlinson, to decode the cuneiform writing of Mesopotamia. Once again the same text appeared in three different languages.

▼ This is an example of Indus Valley script.

The Indus Valley script

So far no one has been able definitely to decode the Indus script, although some people claim to have done so and experts have interpreted some of the signs. You can find out more on page 23.

Seals

What were they made of?

Over 2,000 seals have been found in the Indus Valley. Most of them were about 2.75cm square and made of soapstone, a soft stone that was easily carved using chisels and small drills. After being inscribed the seals were fired to harden them.

▲ *Actual size.*

▲ *This seal was found at Mohenjo-daro.*

◄ *Seals were carved like this at the back, with a hole drilled through, probably to take a cord.*

What were they used for?

The seals were stamps, probably used for trade, perhaps to show the name or rank of a tradesman. We know the Indus people traded valuable goods over long distances because both seals and sealings (clay that has been stamped with a seal) have been found throughout the Indus Valley and further away.

◄ *Clay sealings like this one are evidence of how the seals were used.*

What do they show?

A few seals show people and gods but most show an animal with some script above. Perhaps the animal represents a family group. The writing usually begins above the head of the animal and reads from right to left. You will be able to see this better if you look at the seals in a mirror.

The seals have short inscriptions. The longest has only 17 symbols. People have used computers to analyse the frequency of symbols. The jar symbol is the most common. The fish is also shown frequently, but it does not always look the same. How many jars and fish can you see on the seals on these pages?

◄ *The one-horned animal is the most common image. Seals showing this are found throughout the Indus Valley. The animal might be a symbol belonging to a powerful group of people. What could the object in front of it be?*

What could the inscriptions mean?

Some people think that the fish symbol means 'star', because, in languages that might be like those spoken in the Indus Valley area, the same word is used for 'fish' and 'star'. They also think that the fish combined with other symbols might refer to particular planets or stars, named after gods. (It is known that this happened in other civilisations. We call most of our planets after Greek or Roman gods.) This could mean that religion played some part in the inscriptions on the seals.

Make a seal

Make a seal using clay. Carve out a picture of an animal and your name. Remember you will have to write this backwards.

Decline of the cities

Between about 1900 and 1800 BC many people stopped living in the cities, although northern settlements survived longer than those in the south. We do not know what caused this way of life to end and there are several different opinions.

These are three ideas that people put forward for why the Indus Valley civilisation came to an end.

Environmental changes meant that people could no longer farm efficiently. Also earthquakes caused the river to flood and this meant that people could no longer live in the cities.

The government could no longer rule properly and trade and social organisation just collapsed. The people probably moved away.

I think a powerful army from the west and northwest invaded and destroyed the civilisation.

What evidence do the archaeologists give?

Let's look at the evidence archaeologists give for their opinions. Several archaeologists claim that the poor standard of building on the highest level might be evidence of decline.

In 1931 Sir John Marshall said that animals shown on the seals only live in jungles and there are no jungles in the area now. His idea is that climate change caused the land to become arid; rivers dried up or changed course. People could no longer farm.

In 1965 Dr Dales found evidence that Mohenjo-daro was often buried in silt. The houses were rebuilt on top of old ones. He thought that this showed that the river often flooded.

In 1968 Sir Mortimer Wheeler concluded that the civilisation was destroyed by a well-armed invading force. During excavations, 39 bodies were found in the streets and houses of Mohenjo-daro. They had not been properly buried. Most had died at the same time. Sir Mortimer Wheeler thought they had been massacred.

Archaeologist Sir Mortimer Wheeler (1890-1976).

Excavations in 1979 led Mr Raikes to think that earthquakes near the mouth of the River Indus caused a great lake which flooded Mohenjo-daro every century. Salt from the flood water would have poisoned the soil.

▼ *The mouth of the River Indus today.*

In 1991 Professor Ratnagar suggested that the ruling family might have lost control and fought among themselves. Some broken statues have been found in Mohenjo-daro and Professor Ratnagar wonders if they could have been statues of rulers, smashed to show that the rulers were no longer respected.

You judge

Which archaeologist do you think is right? Could there be some truth in all their statements? Use encyclopedias and other sources of information to find out if Sir John Marshall is right about the animals on the seals.

More questions than answers

We have learnt a lot about the remarkable Indus Valley civilisation. We know that the people were skilled in architecture and engineering and that they traded widely in their own area and overseas. But we do not know what brought about the end of the civilisation and there are many other gaps in our knowledge. Try to answer the questions raised on these two pages, using what you know about the Indus Valley and its people.

Religion

Both gods and goddesses were carved on seals. Archaeologists think people might have used clay figurines when they prayed. Did the people worship a female goddess? If they did, how might this have affected women in the Indus Valley civilisation?

▼ *Some graves have been found lying north to south. Inside the graves were some grave goods. What does that tell us about the people's beliefs?*

▶ *There are several clay figurines dressed like this. She is wearing a large headdress with two panniers.*

Government

Think about the following points and discuss your ideas with a friend.

- There is no obvious 'royal' palace. Many of the buildings in the lower town were larger than those on the Upper Mound.

- There are no rich decorations. Perhaps there were once. We know that the people had gold and silver.

- No burial place of an important person, or memorial to one, has been found. What could this mean?

- Did one person or family rule the entire civilisation? How could that have been organised?

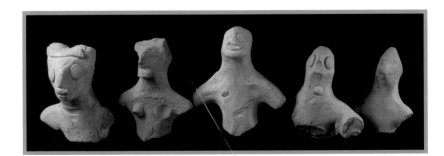

What did they look like?

Skeletons can tell us how tall people were. Otherwise the only evidence of what the people looked like comes from statues and figurines. Many figurines were very roughly made and not like portraits, but they give us some clues about jewellery and headwear. Look closely at some of the photos and see what you can find out.

What were their names?

Perhaps the saddest thing is that we do not know the names of the people who lived here over 4,000 years ago.

◄
► *The figurines on the left don't give us much information, but the woman on the right is holding a baby. What do you think this tells us?*

Knowledge record

Draw up and complete a table like this. Make sure you include everything you know.

The Indus Valley Civilisation

What I know	What I still want to know	Where I can look for information

Glossary

administration — the local government of a city.

alluvium, alluvial — rich soil that is carried by rivers and deposited when they flood.

archaeologists — people who find out about the past by looking at the remains that people have left behind. This includes buildings and tools, as well as animal bones and plant seeds.

arid — very dry. Arid land becomes almost like a desert.

artefacts — man-made objects, for example pottery or tools.

astrology — the belief that stars and planets can influence people's lives.

bitumen — a tar-like substance that is waterproof.

bronze — a mixture of copper and tin.

chisel — a sharp tool used to carve out wood or soapstone.

chute — a sloping channel to drain water.

citadel — a fortress or fortified area of a town. Citadels of the Indus Valley had high, thick walls and towers at each corner.

civilisation — groups of people sometimes living in populated areas that share common features. In the Indus Valley the major towns were built in the same style and a common system of weights was used.

copper — a reddish metal, probably one of the first used by man.

course — the route that a river takes through the land.

cultivate — to prepare the ground for growing crops.

cuneiform — writing used in Mesopotamia, using combinations of wedge-shaped characters.

decline — to deteriorate or get worse. A civilisation declines when it is past its best.

deduction — something worked out by using clues.

durable — hard-wearing and long-lasting.

engineers — people who use knowledge of maths and science in designing and building.

evidence — artefacts or archaeological remains that help to prove or support an idea.

excavate — to dig a large area of land carefully in search of information about the past.

figurine — a small model of a human figure, often made of clay.

fillet — a narrow band, often of metal, that goes around the head.

finds — artefacts and remains found by archaeologists during excavations.

findspots — places where artefacts have been found. Archaeologists make an exact record of where they find everything.

fired — baked to a very high temperature in a kiln.

flood plain — the land on either side of a river which regularly floods.

flourish	to thrive and become wealthy.
granary	a building designed to store grain.
grave goods	objects put in a person's grave to provide for their needs in the afterlife.
hearth	the floor under and around a fire.
hieroglyph	a character used in ancient Egyptian writing.
ideogram	a combination of pictograms, or a pictogram changed to symbolise an idea rather than an object.
inscribe	to cut into the surface of something.
irrigation	watering crops by channelling water along man-made canals.
kiln	an oven for firing bricks and pottery.
massacred	violently killed.
Mesopotamia	'the land between two rivers'. The rivers to which the name refers are the Tigris and Euphrates in Iraq.
Mohenjo-daro	a city of the Indus Valley civilisation. Its name means 'Mound of the Dead'.
monsoon	a strong wind that blows across most of Asia, usually bringing rain.
mud-brick	bricks dried in the sun but not fired in a kiln. These bricks begin to crumble after a few years.
nutrients	minerals in the soil essential for growing crops well.
panniers	deep baskets.
pictogram	a simple shape used to represent an object.

pollen	very fine powder from flowers. It can tell archaeologists which plants used to grow in the region.
ratio	proportion.
rebus	a 'play on words' where a picture can represent a word that it sounds like.
seal	a piece of carved stone used to stamp wet clay.
settlement	the permanent home of a community.
sherd or shard	a broken piece of pottery. Even small pieces tell archaeologists quite a lot.
silt	fine mud or soil left by a river after the flood waters have gone.
sling-shots	round missiles that can be fired from a sling, a little like a catapult, but without elastic.
source	the origin of a river.
subsequent	following or next in a series.
terracotta	clay fired in a kiln so that it is waterproof and does not crumble.
trefoil	a pattern of three leaves.
tributaries	rivers that flow into a larger one.
UNESCO Heritage Site	heritage is what is left of the past. UNESCO (United Nations Educational, Scientific and Cultural Organisation) helps countries to find, protect and preserve their heritage.
water table	a level below which the ground is waterlogged.
yields	the amounts of crops that can be harvested.

For teachers and parents

This book is designed to support and extend the learning objectives for Unit 16 of the QCA History Scheme of Work for Key Stages 1 and 2.

The Indus Valley civilisation is one of the least well-known but most fascinating cultures of the ancient world. There is much evidence of a flourishing and sophisticated society that extended over an area of some 1.25 million square kilometres of modern-day Pakistan and northwest India principally during the fourth, third and second millennia BC. Our knowledge of the people and their way of life comes from extensive archaeology of the area, undertaken over the last 80-100 years. Larger towns were laid out with parallel streets and a highly developed system of drainage. Houses had dedicated bathrooms often emptying directly into the town sewers and some houses had toilets. There were many public and private wells providing drinking water.

An assortment of artefacts has given us an insight into the everyday lives of the people, but the script remains undeciphered although some signs have been interpreted. Consequently we have no definitive knowledge of the system of government or beliefs of the people, although deductions have been made based upon the evidence of artefacts. We do not even know the names of any of the citizens.

The system that unified the Indus civilisation eventually came to an end about the middle of the second millennium BC, but there is nothing to prove that there was a cataclysmic catastrophe. It is known that people exploited new land and developed new farming techniques.

Studying the Indus Valley civilisation gives a unique opportunity to develop children's understanding of chronology and of the range of sources of information available. The questions posed in the text are designed to develop children's historical skills by encouraging them to make use of the evidence available. Therefore, many questions do not have 'right' or 'wrong' answers as the information can be interpreted in different ways.

There are opportunities for cross-curricular work particularly in literacy, mathematics and design and technology. ICT plays a very important part in supporting children's learning as they work through the book.

SUGGESTED FURTHER ACTIVITIES

Pages 4 – 5 Where on earth is the Indus Valley?
To extend the work on these pages you might ask children to:
Compare distances between Indus cities and European cities.

Find European capital cities built on riverbanks.

Write a report to justify building a new settlement close to a riverbank. Children could investigate other features such as climate and topography before compiling their report.

Pages 6 – 7 When did the civilisation flourish?
Make sets of 5 or 6 cards with key events in the development of human society. Let pairs or small groups of children sequence the cards, discussing which events probably predate others. Go through their ideas, asking for their reasoning. Give them approximate dates for each event. Display these on a timeline that goes to the present day, so that children can begin to develop greater awareness of chronology. All dates are approximate.

People used weapons to hunt	pre 30 000 BC
Earliest known cave paintings	30 000 BC
Earliest known rafts	23 000 BC
Earliest known sewing needle	20 000 BC
Bows and arrows first used	9 000 BC
First dogs (wolves) domesticated	9 000 BC
Earliest crop farming	9 000 BC
First goats and sheep domesticated	8 000 BC
First brick dwellings	7 000 BC
First weaving loom used	6 000 BC
Early writing	4 000 BC
First wheel thrown pots	3 750 BC
First wheeled vehicle	3 500 BC
Plough first used in farming	3 000 BC
The Indus Valley Civilisation	2 500 BC
The first paper was made	200 AD

Answers to questions: people would have noticed that crops grown on alluvial deposits gave higher yields than others; people living in cities would have been more interdependent and less self-sufficient for food.

Pages 8 – 9 Meet an archaeologist
To reinforce children's understanding of archaeology, ask each child to decorate a paper plate with a pattern. To make the task harder, ask for a repeating pattern. Cut each plate into several pieces, depending upon the children's ability. Children must write their name on the back of each piece to avoid confusion. Ask another child to reassemble the pieces. Make it harder by removing some of the pieces.

'I'm thinking of a word'. Give children a common letter string. Ask them to write a list of words that start or end with the letter string or contain it in the middle. Why do they not know what word you are thinking of? Uncertainty relates this to archaeology. This activity also links to the symbols on seals as some only appear in certain positions.

Pages 10 – 11 Visiting Mohenjo-daro: the upper town
Take a walk through the remains of Mohenjo-daro: http://www.harappa.com/har/moen0.html. It will be helpful if children have a site plan from which they can identify the major structures.

Explore the remains and identify key features of an Indus settlement: http://www.ancientindia.co.uk/indus/explore/exp_set.html.

Pages 12 – 13 Exploring the lower town
Children could create an interactive dig, using 'hot-spots' on a map of the lower town to take the user to pictures and information about artefacts found there.

Pages 14 – 15 Everyday life in the Indus Valley
The children could use pictures of artefacts to ask and answer questions about everyday life. You will find pictures of artefacts at http://www.ancientindia.co.uk/indus/explore/exp_set.html. Scroll down then click on 'Look through an archaeologist's notebook'. Groups of children could present information, using evidence from artefacts. They could use a branching database to sort and classify artefacts.

Answers on other jobs: as well as skilled craftsmen making bricks, pots and jewellery, there would have been people to design new buildings, maintain fresh supply of water, perhaps regulate trade, and maintain law and order.

Pages 16 – 17 Weights and measures
Children could make the net of an Indus Valley brick. Now make several identical bricks and use them to investigate bonding patterns.

Children could pretend to be an Indus trader. They use the ratio of Indus weights, beginning with 1, each double the mass of the previous one, up to 64. They could find out which weights would be used to weigh, e.g. 37, 84, 120, 19, 5. What is the heaviest mass that could be weighed using only one of each weight? Are there masses less than this that cannot be weighed using only one of each weight?

Answers on other skills: people would need to know how to create right angles and different-shaped bricks for wells.

Pages 18 – 19 Playing detective
Give children pictures of objects with information about their size and the material from which they are made. Let them suggest what each object could be for. The container on page 19 (left) is believed to have been a bird cage. The terracotta triangular cakes may have been used in the same way as a loofah. Archaeologists do not know what the tall containers with holes were used for, but children could be encouraged to use experiences from their own lives to deduce their function.

Pages 20 – 21 The written word
Play Shannon's Game. Create a long sentence with articles and prepositions missing. Ask the children to fill in the gaps, noting the relationship to subsequent words. They could then create their own sentences with parts of speech missing for others to complete. Leading on from this, children could create a piece of text using the pictograms, ideograms and rebus symbols. Discuss which words are easy to represent, which are difficult and which need to be omitted; link this to their understanding of parts of speech. If you omit words, does this mean that different interpretations can be put on the text?

Pages 22 – 23 Seals
You might try one or all of these activities: (1) Share out pictures of seals. Ask the children to identify the frequency of different symbols. They could also look for symbols that commonly come at the end of an inscription, and variations on particular symbols. (2) Give the children drawings of some of the simpler symbols and ask them to suggest some meanings. Discuss these as a class. (3) Can the children identify numbers on the seals? What is the significance, if any, of the different lengths of lines? (4) Look at some of the seals that depict scenes. Ask the children to write legends based on the pictures.

The object in front of the one-horned animal might be a feeding trough.

Pages 24 – 25 Decline of the cities
Divide the class into groups. Each uses resources in the classroom to investigate further the reasons given for the decline of the civilisation. Conduct an enquiry in which each group puts forward their theories, supported with evidence. Which theory (if any) do the children think is most persuasive? Does the fact that Professor Ratnagar's evidence is the most recent give added weight to her ideas? If so, in what ways? Can the children put forward other convincing arguments?

Pages 26 – 27 More questions than answers
Ask the children to find pictures of statues and figurines. What are the similarities and differences? Can the children describe the faces?

Answers to questions: worshipping a goddess would have raised the status of women; the fact that no important grave had been found might mean that everyone was treated equally when they died, or that the graves of important people have not yet been found.

ADDITIONAL RESOURCES

http://www.ancientindia.co.uk/indus/index.html – a site created by staff at the British Museum. The Staffroom contains background information for teachers as well as some worksheets. The Story, Explore and Challenge sections are suitable for children.

http://www.harappa.com contains many images of artefacts and excavated sites; **http://www.harappa.com/teach** has online teaching resources and publications.

A video of programmes made by the BBC for its Primary History series is available from **http://www.bbcschoolshop.com/search.asp**.

http://www.bbc.co.uk/schools/indusvalley/ is a website for children in which they locate and explore Mohenjo-daro in a virtual environment.

THE INDUS VALLEY National Curriculum History KS2 by U. Aafjes & I. Aronovsky, illus. C. Barker (Commonwealth Institute). This resource has extensive information, pictures and activities and is available from **http://www.harappa.com/teach**.

How do we know about the Indus Valley Civilisation? This resource pack including picture cards, a teacher's guide and children's activities is available from **http://www.pcet.co.uk/index.html**.

Index